the
LEARNING &
DEVELOPMENT
BOOK
change the way you think about L&D

the
LEARNING &
DEVELOPMENT
BOOK change the way you think about L&D

Tricia Emerson
Mary Stewart

ASTD
WORKPLACE LEARNING & PERFORMANCE
PRESS

1640 King Street Box 1443
Alexandria, VA 22313-1443 USA

t: 800.628.2783   703.683.8100
f: 703.683.8103   www.astd.org

ASTD Press is an internationally renowned source of insightful and practical information on workplace learning and performance topics, including training basics, evaluation and return-on-investment, instructional systems development, e-learning, leadership, and career development.

Ordering Information: Books published by ASTD Press can be purchased by visiting ASTD's website at store.astd.org or by calling 800.628.2783 or 703.683.8100.

Library of Congress Control Number: 2011928868

ISBN-10: 1-56286-808-X
ISBN-13: 978-1-56286-808-6

ASTD Press Editorial Staff:
Director: Anthony Allen
Manager, ASTD Press: Larry Fox
Community of Practice Managers:
 Juana Llorens, Kristin Husak, Justin Brusino
Associate Editor: Ashley McDonald
Associate Editor: Heidi Smith
Editorial Assistant: Stephanie Castellano

Copyeditors: Larry Fox, Stephanie Castellano,
 Heidi Smith
Graphic Design: Yvette Tam
Interior Illustration: Ramiro Alonso, Colleen Coover
Printed by: Versa Press, Inc., East Peoria, Illinois;
www.versapress.com

CONTENTS

LEARNING AND DEVELOPMENT

is hard. Even for us, the learning and development professionals. As we help people blossom, we must continually sharpen our own skills.

We wrote this book for people like us – experienced, time-challenged professionals looking for ways to be more effective. The insights in this book are meant to help when you feel stalled. They are about the gotchas – the hard-won knowledge that comes from skinned knees and bumped heads. They might jump-start your creativity, give you a fresh idea, remind you of something that worked in the past, or simply change your perspective.

You enable effective learning. And from time to time, you must articulate the case for effective learning practices. This book gives you simple ideas and concepts to illustrate these needs and illuminate learning and development efforts for you, your clients, your teams and your company leadership.

This book is simple and flexible. Our chapters are written to be short and easy to digest. Each contains a "nugget of wisdom" from years of learning and development consulting experience. There's no need to start at the beginning. Read the table of contents and pick something that interests you. Each chapter is self-contained, so read one or read them all, in any order you like.

Periodically, a chapter will give you suggestions:

 This icon indicates a suggestion – other chapters, related to the current topic, that you might want to read.

 Want to learn more about the topic? This icon references books, articles, and websites that will help you "go deep."

FOREWORD

Here's a test I used to evaluate the *Learning and Development Book*: As a researcher I believe in stratified random sampling. So I flipped to two random pages from each of the four sections. I reviewed the content to see if I could immediately apply the concepts, principles, and procedures to designing and delivering training. The answer was yes on all eight occasions. Conclusion: This is a practical book with ready-to-use (and self-contained) ideas.

Here's the second test I performed: I flipped through the pages looking for any evaluation checklist. I am a great believer in authors walking the talk. So I applied the six-item checklist on page 15 to determine whether the book is "highly evolved." It sure is. It fulfills a need, it is relevant, it acknowledges the reader's background, it requires and rewards readers for taking responsibility, it respects the reader, and it is flexible enough to accommodate different learning styles. I also used another checklist, on page 39, to see whether the book incorporates elements of engagement. It sure does. It is extremely realistic and provides details at a level appropriate to the reader. There are plenty of opportunities for the reader to practice, and it effectively prepares the reader to perform as a facilitative trainer.

The book is informal, friendly, and playful. It is an easy read (even to non-native speakers like me). It is nicely illustrated with relevant pictures, tables, graphic organizers, and charts.

I do have a major regret about the book. I wish it were around 40 years earlier, when I started my career as a trainer. I am sure I would have benefitted more from reading this book than those three graduate level courses I took…on adult learning theory and models, transformational learning, and post-modern perspectives on adult education. So if I ever invent a time machine, I'll send Trish and Mary back to 1971.

Sivasailam "Thiagi" Thiagarajan
The Thiagi Group, Bloomington, IN

ACKNOWLEDGEMENTS

One winter, our team of practitioners shared some downtime sitting around a table and chatting about our client experiences. We realized that this lull in our workload was a wonderful opportunity to capture the best of what this group, some of the finest in the field, knew about learning.

The group took on the task to "riff" on their expertise. "Don't write the basics," Trish said. "Write for people like yourselves: short on time, short on attention, but deep in expertise." They did. And then Trish and Mary added more and made sense of the output.

This book is the result of that labor. We worked on it monthly during company meetings for two years, and periodically in between. And while the content and form evolved during this time, the heart of it would not exist except for the efforts of the following contributors:

Dorian Adam	**Rebecca Spiros**
Farrow Adamson	**Mark Webster**
Chris Harper	**Yvette Tam,** *Designer*
Hastie Afkhami	**Ramiro Alonso,** *Illustrator*
Kim Lewis	**Colleen Coover,** *Illustrator*
Jane Munagian	**Carol Irvine,** *Photographer*
Tina Richards	**Genevieve Shiffrar,** *Photographer*
Bettina Rousos	

Thanks to these people, and the entire Emerson Human Capital team, for their contribution, faith, and diligence, particularly when they were also juggling client obligations. Working with them remains one of our greatest joys!

Trish Emerson and Mary Stewart

ONE MORE THING...

We'd like to introduce Edie.

Edie is the personification of the perfect learning and development professional.

> Thank you.

We'll use her to deliver some of the lessons of this book.

> I beg your pardon. 'Use me?'

Sorry. We're honored that she's agreed to come to life on our pages to impart her incomparable wisdom.

> Indeed.

No really, she's miraculous.

> That'll do, thank you.

SECTION 1
Fundamentals

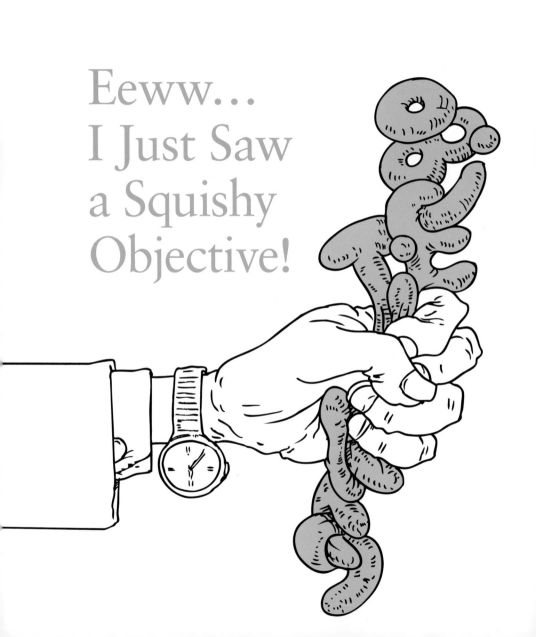

Eeww...
I Just Saw
a Squishy
Objective!

Weak learning objectives slip through our fingers like mud. And they can ruin a training program.

Ruin it? What's the big deal?
Writing learning objectives isn't just a semantic exercise. Objectives are the foundation of our training. They define the behavior we expect learners to perform and allow us to measure that behavior. They help us determine whether training is working.

What's wrong with these objectives?
"At the end of this module, you will:

+ know the steps for making a transfer.

+ understand the importance of maintaining a safe
  work environment."

Right. Squishy. How can we observe someone "knowing" or "understanding"? How will they *show us* that they know or understand?

Objectives must be observable and measurable.
This is especially hard for instructor-led, presentation-based courses. But don't worry; invariably there is a behavior that will allow us to measure the degree to which the participant has learned that important information. Find it and build it into the learning objective.

ACTION VERBS

Avoid squishy words that don't describe a behavior. If you can't see it or hear it, it isn't a good word to use. Try words like these:

arrange
create
define
demonstrate
describe
identify
measure
rank
solve
use
write

Edie Says: Bloom determined that certain verbs indicate different levels of content mastery. For example, describing an accounting principle is a lower-level skill than evaluating the principle or contrasting it with another.

BLOOM'S TAXONOMY VERBS

KNOWLEDGE	Count, Define, Describe, Draw, Find, Identify, Label, List, Match, Name, Quote, Recall, Recite, Sequence, Tell, Write
COMPREHENSION	Conclude, Demonstrate, Discuss, Explain, Generalize, Identify, Illustrate, Interpret, Paraphrase, Predict, Report, Restate, Review, Summarize, Tell
APPLICATION	Apply, Change, Choose, Compute, Dramatize, Interview, Prepare, Produce, Role-play, Select, Show, Transfer, Use
ANALYSIS	Analyze, Characterize, Classify, Compare, Contrast, Debate, Deduce, Diagram, Differentiate, Discriminate, Distinguish, Examine, Outline, Relate, Research, Separate
SYNTHESIS	Compose, Construct, Create, Design, Develop, Integrate, Invent, Make, Organize, Perform, Plan, Produce, Propose, Rewrite
EVALUATION	Appraise, Argue, Assess, Choose, Conclude, Critique, Decide, Evaluate, Judge, Justify, Predict, Prioritize, Prove, Rank, Rate, Select

THE BCDs OF OBJECTIVES

To be effective, an objective should define:

THE DESIRED BEHAVIOR THE LEARNER WILL PERFORM.

THE CONDITIONS UNDER WHICH THE PERFORMANCE WILL HAPPEN.

THE DEGREE TO WHICH SUCCESSFUL BEHAVIOR IS DEFINED.

For example:

WHEN YOU **SEE A SMALL FIRE** (conditions) YOU WILL BE ABLE TO USE A FIRE EXTINGUISHER TO **EXTINGUISH** (behavior) THE FIRE **COMPLETELY,** THE **FIRST TIME** (degree).

Take the Learner's Perspective : pg 124
PowerPoint Is Not Training : pg 36
How Do You Know Learners Met Their Objectives : pg 24

MAKE IT WORK

You have been given these objectives for a training module. Fix them!

UNDERSTAND HOW TO OPERATE A SEWING MACHINE.

KNOW WHOM TO CONTACT WHEN YOU HAVE QUESTIONS.

PROVIDE DETAILS ABOUT THE NEW PROCESS.

LEARN THE PROPER WAY TO PUT MERCHANDISE ON THE SHELF.

To learn more, see:
Mager, Robert F. (1984). *Preparing Instructional Objectives.*
Belmont, CA: Lake Publishing Company

Bloom, B. S. (ed.) (1956) *Taxonomy of Educational
Objectives, the Classification of Educational Goals.*
New York: McKay

Critical.
Common.
Catastrophic.

Don't train everything

It's overwhelming, ineffective and costly.

CRITICAL: What are the most important things for the employee to do? What are the essentials?

COMMON: What will he or she have to do most often? What is an everyday task?

CATASTROPHIC: What will shut down the business, lose clients, cause injury, or invite a lawsuit?

Make Sure They Can Do These Things : pg 24

LET'S USE YOUR TEETH AS AN EXAMPLE

CRITICAL: IDENTIFY THE ELEMENTS OF ORAL HYGIENE
COMMON: DEMONSTRATE EFFECTIVE BRUSHING TECHNIQUE
CATASTROPHIC: IDENTIFY SIGNS OF DISEASE AND TOOTH DECAY

HOW ABOUT A BUSINESS EXAMPLE?

CRITICAL: CLOSE THE BOOKS EACH MONTH
COMMON: POST AN ITEM TO THE GENERAL LEDGER
CATASTROPHIC: IDENTIFY AND FIX A
POORLY DEFINED CHART OF ACCOUNTS

M	MATURE CONTENT
	SOPHISTICATED LEARNING PROGRAM

A	ACTIVE ENGAGING AND PERFORMANCE-BASED

E	EVERYONE 
	EFFECTIVE FOR ALL LEARNERS

Make Sure Your Training Is Rated "Mature"

Imagine an instructor bringing his participants into a session and writing his name on the blackboard. Participants take out their text books and read a passage. Then the instructor lectures for 40 minutes, stopping only to quiz the class on what he's said.

You'd never design training like that, right? To be successful, your learning program must be more sophisticated.

Edie Says: Between us, dear, 'Adult Learning Theory' is so last season! Yes, we're talking about Adult Learning Theory but the way people commonly define it – juxtaposed with pedagogy – is dated. Children and adults do learn differently, but not the way we were taught in grad school. Both audiences need engagement. Now pedagogy is more focused on brain development, which enables aptitude, which is where the field should be. So, the principles we present in the chapter are not really about Adult Learning Theory – they are about creating a positive learning environment, which applies to adults and children alike.

Play Works : pg 95
PowerPoint Is Not Training : pg 36
Presentation or Facilitation : pg 71

IS YOUR LEARNING PROGRAM HIGHLY EVOLVED?

1. **NEED** | People are goal-oriented. Provide a problem to solve, a task to master, or a life issue to address.

2. **RELEVANCE** | Show learners the "What's in it for me?" Point out benefits important to them. Use specific examples of job performance benefits, career advancement, smoother teamwork, and easier customer interactions.

3. **ACKNOWLEDGEMENT** | Learners bring a rich background to learning situations. They will be more motivated to learn if you acknowledge – and provide them opportunities to share – their knowledge and experience.

4. **RESPONSIBILITY** | People prefer to take responsibility for their own learning. Make them full participants by giving them as many choices as possible about what to learn and how to learn it.

5. **RESPECT** | Learners take mistakes personally. Don't make them afraid of judgment or ridicule. Maintain a welcoming atmosphere where participants are free to give opinions and ask questions.

6. **STYLE** | Everyone has a preferred learning style. Some people like to read, others learn best by listening, and others prefer hands-on learning. Some are visual, some verbal, some physical. Try to allow for all styles in the course of the training program.

Are You Lost?

Where am I?
What am I doing?
Where am I going?
What are you **talking about?**

These are the questions of a very confused person, right? They are, all too often, the questions of learners in training courses. What can we do to help these lost souls? We can start by providing our learners **advance organizers**.

An **advance organizer** is framework that helps the learner interpret and classify incoming information. It could be a story, a list of steps or a flowchart, a conceptual model, or a timeline. It gives **context** and **position**.

Think of it like a map. A map shows a picture or diagram of the entire environment, then says "You Are Here."

Edie Says: Psst… let me equip you to discuss advance organizers as if you're a PhD in instructional design. We'll cover their history from beginning, middle, to end.

Beginning: based on research by the FAMOUS Jean Piaget, who studied his own children to determine how the brain stores information.

Middle: developed by David Ausubel in 1960 as frameworks for processing and storing new information.

End: validated by researchers as an effective way to improve understanding and recall!

Advance organizers give learners the big picture, the roadmap, the outline. They are training's 'you are here' sign, and they have other benefits too.

Let's look at two types of advance organizers: narrative and graphic.

Why are we making this change?

How will we do it?

What are our next steps?

NARRATIVE ORGANIZERS PRESENT THE NEW INFORMATION TO THE LEARNER IN THE FORM OF A STORY

Listen carefully to an exceptional public speaker sometime. Good speakers understand the power of story and use stories to give their listeners the framework they need to absorb the message.

◆ **Well-known stories, like fairy tales and shared history, work because everyone is familiar with them.** As the speaker tells each part of the story, as an introduction to content, learners have an instant sense of where they are in the session. Recall is better because they'll attach content to something they already know. There's a bonus: the speaker can use a metaphor to reinforce learning. ("Little Red Riding Hood" is about avoiding hidden danger; "Hansel and Gretel" is about being lost and finding your way home.)

◆ **Personal stories are effective because they help learners relate the content to their own experiences.** As the instructor talks about his/her own life, learners remember similar situations. This aids recall and reinforces the connection between instructor and learner. They also provide opportunities for humor, which helps retention as well.

◆ **Case studies can serve as organizers and also carry content.** At each step in the story, the learner hears about a real-life challenge and how it was solved.

Stories Are Powerful Learning Tools : pg 78

Edie Says: Narrative organizers are some of my very favorite organizers! Here's an example.

Example

Let's say I want to teach three principles of a successful IT implementation: "Make them fall in love with the new technology," "Choose the smart solution," and "Be willing to do the hard work." I could use the classic story "The Wizard of Oz" as an organizer. As I go through the course, I touch on the story as I introduce each concept:

DOROTHY MEETS THE SCARECROW, WHO WISHES HE HAD A HEART: "MAKE THEM FALL IN LOVE WITH THE NEW TECHNOLOGY."

DOROTHY MEETS THE TIN MAN, WHO WISHES HE HAD A BRAIN: "CHOOSE THE SMART SOLUTION."

DOROTHY MEETS THE LION, WHO WISHES HE HAD COURAGE: "BE WILLING TO DO THE HARD WORK."

The narrative organizer serves two purposes in this case. It is a **roadmap**, orienting the learner. People know this story, so they know that when Dorothy meets the Tin Man, they're about halfway through the content. It is also a **content reinforcer**. It might be hard for a learner to remember my three concepts on their own, but everyone remembers the Scarecrow, Tin Man, and Lion. From those familiar characters, it's a short mental step to recalling the principles I've taught.

GRAPHIC ORGANIZERS SET UP
OR OUTLINE THE NEW INFORMATION

Many people will tell you they are "visual learners." Graphics provide schema that instantly make sense to us.

♦ **Timelines** give information about where learners are in the session or where they would be in a typical work day. These are very basic organizers, and sometimes simpler is better.

♦ **Lists of work steps** give time cues but also carry content. They double as organizers and job aids, so that learners can use the same vehicle back in their real-life environments. This helps them recall information and skills they learned during training.

♦ **Flowcharts** are similar to lists, but are more graphic. Flowcharts can also accommodate multiple timelines and directions, whereas lists are purely linear.

♦ **Maps** are great for a complex situation, where we want learners to understand all elements of the "landscape," even if it's conceptual, then choose "where to go" to apply their skills.

♦ **Conceptual models** have many of the same benefits, but are not tied to time, nor are they necessarily linear. As the instructor presents, he or she can move around the model as the content requires. Models are great for teaching "what if" scenarios, where participants must decide which strategy or tool to use, given a set of conditions.

1. TIMELINE

Chill Bill's Ice Cream | A Day in the Store

9:00 am --> Complete Store Open Checklist

9:30 am --> Complete Counter Open Checklist

9:55 am --> Taste Ice Cream

10:00 am --> Open Store

2. WORK STEPS

Chill Bill's Ice Cream | Opening the Counter

- Set the freezer temperature
- Draw smiley face on condensation
▷ • Buff the cherries
- Dust the nuts

3. FLOWCHART

Chill Bill's Ice Cream | How to create that split is bananas

- Drizzle should always be stored at room temperature.
- Shake the bottle! Nobody likes a gloopy drizzle.
- Drizzle fights are not encouraged.

4. MAP

Chill Bill's Ice Cream | Store Map

5. CONCEPTUAL MODEL

Chill Bill's Ice Cream | Customer Loyalty

Training Was a Success

How do you know?

You don't, for sure, unless you measure it. But how? Donald Kirkpatrick proposed five levels of evaluation, which have been widely adopted to assess training success.

LEVEL 1 measures **reaction** to the course. Participants complete a survey, sometimes called a "smile sheet." It's cheap; it's easy; it's not very meaningful. But it can be used to tweak the session and eliminate elements that participants dislike.

LEVEL 2 measures **learning** in the training environment. Participants take a test at the end of a module or session, sometimes paired with a pre-test for comparison. This is great for technical skills, especially those taught via computer. But it's tough to accurately measure learning for anything complex (combining technical and interpersonal skills). And some skills must be performed in a real-world context to be measured in a valid way.

LEVEL 3 measures **application** on the job. The question is whether skills learned transfer to the job setting. Journals or self-administered checklists are good for application tests. Supervisors may observe and coach employees, gather feedback from teammates and customers, and measure error rates and performance against individual metrics or standards.

LEVEL 4 measures **business performance**. These evaluations often mark a shift from individual performance (level 3) to measurement of group performance. These might be in the form of higher sales, customer service data, or product performance. These evaluations often shift from measurement of individual performance to measurement of group performance.

LEVEL 5 measures **return on the training investment** for the business. The challenge is to compare the full cost of training (materials, technology, travel, work-hours, development costs, licensing, entertainment…) with dollars generated because of the training. Returns might be in the form of profit or cost avoidance.

Example | **DRIVER'S EDUCATION**

Speedborough County has introduced a new
high school drivers education program.
It includes instructor-led content, simulation,
and road work. The county wants to know
whether its training investment was
worthwhile. How might we evaluate it?

REACTION | Ask the student how he liked his instructor. Ask him how effective the course was.

LEARNING | Put the student through a road test with an evaluator. If the student gets his license, training was a success!

APPLICATION | Test the driver in real driving conditions, without an instructor or driving tester. Measures might include reduction in moving violations or number of driving hours without an accident.

PERFORMANCE | Look at data like number of accidents, fatalities or speeding violations for all drivers in the county under a certain age.

RETURN ON THE TRAINING INVESTMENT | Compare all costs of training (development, equipment, incremental work-hours) with all dollar benefits (reductions in law enforcement dollars, reduction in medical costs absorbed by the county, insurance and medical savings by individuals that trickle into the local economy).

ORGANIZATIONS DON'T USUALLY MEASURE LEVELS 3, 4 AND 5. WHY?

♦ **NOBODY REALLY NEEDS TO KNOW.**

Sometimes employees are trained in order to satisfy government requirements or to prevent lawsuits or other forms of company losses. If the goal of training is not to improve performance or increase profits, there's little focus on measuring its success.

♦ **LET'S BE HONEST. *WE* DON'T WANT TO DO IT.**

The outcomes are unpredictable. It's like that saying of trial attorneys: "Don't ask a question if you don't already know the answer." We're pretty sure we can get a high rating on a smile sheet, but business performance? ROI? Those are subject to myriad influences.

And evaluation begs the question, "So what?" What will we do with the results? Good or bad, there is an implied action/response. We might need to redesign and redevelop. We might need to fire someone, or take some remedial action. Maybe we trained to the wrong objectives altogether. Who needs it?

Negative results might cause a lot of pain and sink future efforts and budgets. So we often avoid evaluation of our own programs unless sponsors demand it.

Edie Says:
Now, that should settle those pesky accountability issues!

♦ **IT'S EXPENSIVE**

Evaluation costs a lot, and companies generally aren't willing to pay for it. Even training systems with huge costs, like virtual training used by the military, often lack the evaluation that would justify their cost.

That's because, beyond Level 2 ("learning"), evaluation requires observation or monitoring of worker performance. These are extremely expensive. So companies are willing to trust that a link exists between those last three levels: learning, business performance and ROI.

Companies also rely on anecdotal evidence of increased individual team performance post-training.

♦ **IT'S DIFFICULT**

Sound evaluation requires thoughtful instrument development. Evaluators have to be trained or hired, data analyzed, and variable causes isolated and accounted for. Test items must be valid and reliable. Performance criteria must be identified and agreed upon.

Doing all this well requires expertise, effort, time, patience and money.

SO WHY DO IT?

More organizations are demanding it. We might as well be ready to deliver.

It's a competitive edge. Knowing how to evaluate training will put us ahead of the competition. ROI and demonstrable value are huge selling points to sponsors.

It will improve our training. Learning what translates into benefits and what doesn't will make us more successful in the long run.

Edie Says: Let's agree to focus on one result that cost-justifies our course, and measure one or two behaviors associated with it.

We'll tell our boss we're just curious…

Can Your Culture Sabotage Training Success : pg 135

reference

Phillips, Jack. *Handbook of Training Evaluation and Measurement Methods*. Houston: Gulf Professional Publishing, 1997.

Phillips, Jack, and Ron Stone. *How to Measure Training Results: A Practical Guide to Tracking the Six Key Indicators*. New York: McGraw-Hill, 2002.

Kirkpatrick, D.L. *Evaluating Training Programs*. San Francisco: Berrett-Koehler, 1998.

SECTION 2
Medium

An Inconvenient Truth: Powerpoint is Not Training

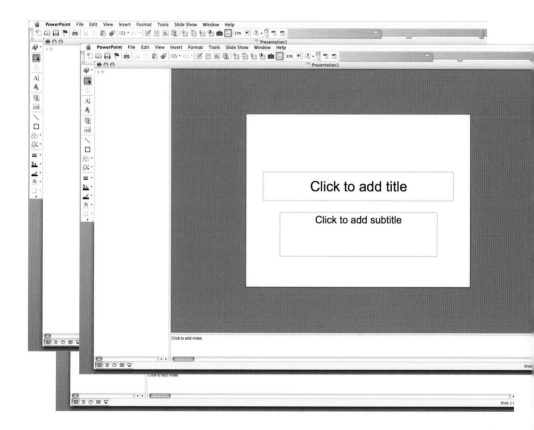

PowerPoint is not training, my friend…

Wait a minute…Al Gore did it. Why can't I?

In his PowerPoint presentation in *An Inconvenient Truth*, Gore shows the gruesome realities facing our planet in hopes we will change our behavior. Al Gore raised awareness about a global crisis. But what he did was not training.

PowerPoint is a great tool for delivering information, especially if we have a stellar speaker. PowerPoint alone, however, is information without action.

If you rely on information alone, don't expect learners to act on what they've heard. Don't expect performance. They need behavior and repetition. They need practice in a safe environment. Only then will they be able to turn our information into results.

> "Beware of the man who works hard to learn something, learns it, and finds himself no wiser than before."
>
> – KURT VONNEGUT, JR.

ELEMENTS OF ENGAGEMENT

CONTENT

- ☐ Is it relevant to expected performance?
- ☐ Is it realistic?
- ☐ Do learners understand why they are learning it?
- ☐ Is the content sequenced logically?
- ☐ Is the detail appropriate for the learner's level?

PERFORMANCE

- ☐ Are there opportunities for learners to practice?
- ☐ Do learners receive relevant feedback when they practice?
- ☐ Do the presentation methods match performance expectations?
- ☐ Does the learning environment model the performance environment?
- ☐ Does the learning prepare for performance?

Trainers and SMEs Are Not the Same Thing : pg 141
Learning Begins When Training Ends : pg 63
Presentation or Facilitation : pg 71

A MULTI-NATIONAL BANK brought an outsourced call center in-house, hiring 25 new team members to handle inbound and outbound calls. They had planned to use existing education materials. The bank had six weeks of instructional content and little time before the center opened. The temptation was to power through the content, delivered via Powerpoint and subject-matter experts. Emerson Human Capital was asked to review the program and recommend a better way.

Edie Says:
Of course I make it look easy. That's my job.

USING A RAPID INSTRUCTIONAL DESIGN APPROACH, THE TEAM DISTILLED TRAINING TO ITS ESSENCE. DESIGNING WHILE THE COURSE WAS BEING DELIVERED, THEY:

CREATED CONTEXT FOR THE PARTICIPANTS BY FRAMING THE CONTENT AND THE OBJECTIVES.

INCORPORATED EXAMPLES AND NON-EXAMPLES TO ILLUSTRATE KEY POINTS.

SEQUENCED THE CONTENT SO LEARNERS GOT THE RIGHT INFORMATION AT THE RIGHT TIME.

ENGAGED PARTICIPANTS BY ADDING MEANINGFUL PRACTICE OPPORTUNITIES.

THE RESULT

The new contact center opened on time with a prepared team who successfully answered client calls representing millions of dollars.

Case Study

Take Vanilla
Off the Menu

What is "vanilla"?

Vanilla means off-the-shelf training. It is:

Built to cover a wide variety of jobs, industries and business problems.

Advertised as "ready to use."

Appealing because it's less expensive than developing from scratch.

Why does "vanilla" leave a bad taste in our mouths? Because it doesn't teach learners to do their jobs. It doesn't:

Use relevant or specific examples from the learner's job or role, so it won't be realistic.

Consider the cultural nuances of the organization.

Test whether the learners will be able to perform differently when they're back on the job.

Yield the changes in performance and business results we expect. In other words, it wastes time and money.

THERE ARE THREE WAYS TO ADD FLAVOR

Once we have a thorough understanding of your audience and its training needs, choose an approach.

Edie Says: PLEASE! I would never settle for vanilla!

1. **CREATE UNIQUE LEARNING.** Start from scratch to meet our specific needs.

2. **CUSTOMIZE.** Buy off-the-shelf and spice it up. *Start by recognizing that no off-the-shelf solution is a perfect fit. We must redesign, edit or supplement existing materials to meet our needs. We can make big changes, using their template as the starting point, or we can make small changes by adding relevant examples.*

3. **BLEND.** Mix and match! *Some elements of a course might be fine as they are. Some might need customization or development from scratch.*

SOME CHANGES TO CONSIDER

Make sure that activities allow participants to **practice** what they'll need to do on the job.

Use case studies and job scenarios that are **specific** to your industry and organization.

Change and add visuals so the **images** are culturally appropriate to your learners.

Build in time for participants to **share ideas** and tips with each other. They'll help bridge the gap between training and their real-life jobs.

Incorporate follow-up sessions and on-the-job **support**, so the learning is reinforced after training is over.

Use what you've got! Leverage **what works** in your organization to enhance training. Consider training methods, setting, style, instructors, communications and organization events.

practice
specific
images
share ideas
support
what works

The Medium
Matters

You wouldn't eat spaghetti with only a spoon, would you?

Training media fit the situation just like a utensil fits a meal. Choose poorly, and you're in for a frustrating experience.

Why Can't We Just Use PowerPoint? : pg 36
Take the User's Perspective : pg 124
Try A Blended Solution : pg 56
Does This Have To Be Boring? : pg 88

THE RIGHT WAY TO CHOOSE

SKILLS | What kind of performance are we teaching? What is the real-life setting? Train in a realistic environment, with realistic tools, so that participants can demonstrate mastery and then transfer it back to the job. If we're training technical skills, that means using the computer system during training. If it's soft skills – well, it's hard to teach facilitation skills via web-based training.

GOALS | What do we need to accomplish? Do we need to check learner performance at the end of training? Do we want training to achieve anything other than skill building (like developing team relationships or creating a positive emotion)?

LEARNERS | Are they new or veterans? Top performers or a mixed bag? Technically skilled or not? Make sure the methods fit.

BUDGET | Can we afford a road show? Can we afford high development costs, up-front? Cost sometimes influences strategy.

LOGISTICS | Where are our learners and how many? Where is our training team and how many? What's needed to support each session? These factors might suggest a method.

Edie Says: **THE WRONG WAY TO CHOOSE**

Web-based training is the latest thing. Everyone's doing it.

Our people are used to instructor-led training.

Computer-based training will be easier for us to maintain.

We have a big pool of facilitators with nothing to do.

These are certainly considerations, but not compelling enough to guide one's choice of training method.

TIPS FOR SELECTING MEDIA

Classroom or instructor-led training (ILT) is best for:

♦ Soft skills like influencing, communication, motivating, presenting, etc.

♦ Training goals that include emotional connection, like team-building or mentoring

♦ An audience with similar skill sets (e.g., newly promoted employees)

♦ An audience grouped in one location or close in proximity

Web based training (WBT) or self-study is best for:

♦ Hard skills like computer-based tasks, financial or safety procedures, operational process, etc.

♦ Training that does not require participant interactivity

♦ Dispersed audience/tight budget *

♦ Mandatory training that requires legal record-keeping

Virtual training (combining virtual ILT and WBT) is best for:

♦ Training that combines soft and hard skills

♦ Training that requires participant and facilitator interactivity (achieved through webinars, web conferences, teleconferences)

♦ Dispersed audience/tight budget *

WBT and virtual training have high production and start-up costs, but overall project expense is often lower due to dollars saved in payroll, travel and lodging.

SELECT MEDIA EARLY

Content development is highly dependent on the medium, so choose it as soon as you know the audience and your training objectives.

A big-four consulting firm used to conduct an annual face-to-face learning experience for top-performing managers and senior consultants. In 2009, due to economic pressures, they opted for a virtual learning experience.

The firm selected a virtual medium consisting of:

- A STRUCTURED 14-HOUR EXPERIENCE SPANNING FOUR WEEKS. THE COURSE PROMOTED NETWORKING AND BUILDING INDUSTRY AND SECTOR KNOWLEDGE.

- INTERACTIVE LEARNING ACTIVITIES USING VARIOUS MODALITIES (PODCASTS, WEBINARS, WIKIS, ETC.). ACTIVITIES REQUIRED A THREE-STEP PROCESS: KNOWLEDGE SHARE, VIRTUAL TEAMWORK, AND AN OUTPUT OR REPORT-OUT.

- ◆ VIRTUAL WORK TEAMS OF SIX TO EIGHT PARTICIPANTS
  THAT WORK TOGETHER ON PROJECTS AND ASSIGNMENTS
  THROUGHOUT THE FOUR WEEKS.

- ◆ COACHES ASSIGNED TO THE WORK TEAMS TO CREATE
  AN INTIMATE LEARNING ENVIRONMENT AND ENCOURAGE
  A HIGH LEVEL OF ENGAGEMENT THROUGHOUT THE
  PROGRAM.

- ◆ PEER AND COACH RECOGNITION THROUGHOUT
  THE PROGRAM.

Once the media were decided, the team designed content around
each training objective. Design and development would have been
very different if the medium were ILT or WBT alone.

A Blended
Solution

Blending makes it smoother

In recent years, learning professionals have been talking about blended learning as if it were something new. But this is the only way people learn. We don't just attend a suite of classroom sessions and come out at the end perfect performers. We learn in multiple ways and the best learning professionals capitalize on this fact.

In practice, blending usually includes face-to-face sessions and computer-delivered content – eLearning, simulations, virtual networking or other web technologies. The instructional designer can choose the best training method for each skill and each type of content, making learning more effective.

Beyond effectiveness, blended learners are happy learners because they are more in charge. Learners select the pace and amount of content for each experience. Learners find that blended programs go down more smoothly.

WHY CAN'T WE JUST MAKE IT ALL VIRTUAL?
WON'T THAT WORK TOO?

Well, it certainly can. But sometimes there's no substitute for meeting face-to-face to practice a skill or watch someone perform a task. And some learning objectives, like building teams or facilitating, require human interaction.

Edie Says: Is it just me or do others have an aversion to all-virtual training? Years ago, I attended an Elliott Massey presentation. He asked the audience, a highly experienced group of instructional designers, how many of them had designed online training. All raised their hands. Then he asked how many had actually taken an online course, as a participant. Only a couple raised their hands. For whatever reason, we opt out of virtual learning when we can. It's just not an exciting prospect. No, dear, your online course is no different. The key to my success has been integration of different delivery methods.

THE INGREDIENTS

SET UP | Provide an overview of the course, including the participant's interaction with media. This is especially helpful for people who have never used blended learning.

PRESENT | Provide context and content through lecture, reading, eLearning and other presentation methods.

DEMONSTRATE | Use simulations, live demonstrations and other methods to illustrate the content.

PRACTICE | Allow the learner to practice using the content in a realistic but controlled environment.

ASSESS | Verify that the learner has mastered the content through certification, performance assessment or informal learning checks.

ASSIST | Provide ongoing support to ensure performance stays on track.

COACH | Make managers and peers part of the program. They should provide ongoing coaching and feedback, and hone learner performance.

COLLABORATE | Build communities of practice that allow for groups of learners to deepen their skills and improve performance over time.

MMMMM, IT'S BLENDED!

A blended learning solution:

- ◆ Reduces costs. Travel, entertainment and sometimes payroll costs are lower.

- ◆ Helps eliminate distance barriers. Learners can meet at least some objectives wherever and whenever they like.

- ◆ Improves satisfaction. Learners who experience variety and feel in charge are happier and more engaged.

Learning Often Happens Outside a Classroom : pg 63
The Medium Really Matters : pg 49

TRY THESE PROPORTIONS:

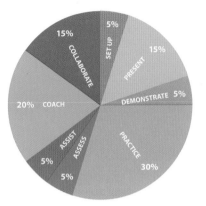

references

Cross, J (2007). *Informal Learning.* San Francisco: Pfeiffer.

Woodall, D (2007). "Blended Learning Solutions for Smaller Companies." http://www.bizlibrary.com/portals/0/Blended-LearningSolutionsforSmallerCompanies.pdf

To learn more, see:
Bersin, Josh. *The Blended Learning Book.*
San Francisco: Pfeiffer, 2004.

Learning Begins When Training Ends

You mean they didn't learn anything in training?

No, that's not what we mean. But nothing focuses the mind like being in the chair, on the job, and having people depend on you.

Even if training is great, the team won't fully learn how to do their jobs until day one. That's when they'll take what they remember from training and try to apply it to real co-workers, real data, and real customers. That's when they'll learn to do it the new way.

Or not! When faced with a ringing phone or a quota or a deadline, will they do things the way they were trained? They might return to old methods or develop work-arounds just to get through the day.

WHAT CAN YOU DO?

Prepare the business for delays. Set stakeholders' and customers' expectations about how significant the change is. Overstaff the team in order to bridge the gap between the old way and the new.

Test knowledge and performance. Do it at the end of training, prior to Day One, and/or after the change is implemented. The more levels of evaluation we use, the more confidence we can have in performance.

Build in performance support. If the change involves a new tool or system, build in help and easy-access answers.

Provide on-the-spot help. People usually have a preferred place to go when they don't know what to do. It might be other teammates, the IT department, the project team, their manager, their trainer, their training materials or reference guides. Use the channel they like to provide answers and support.

Hold on-the-job learning sessions. Build in time, after the change is in place, to learn how to perform better and more efficiently.

Conduct "a-ha" sessions to share tips and support. Get the most out of the change by letting people help each other. Ask people to collect ideas they'd like to share with others and present them to the group.

IMAGINE YOU'RE AT WORK. YOU'RE TRYING TO DO SOMETHING NEW AND YOU GET STUCK. WHO, OR WHAT WILL YOU TURN TO? YOUR BOSS? THAT ONE CO-WORKER WHO ALWAYS HAS THE ANSWERS? IT SUPPORT? REFERENCE GUIDES?

USE THAT. BE WHERE THEY'RE ALREADY GOING.

If learners tend to rely on co-workers, make sure you create super-users nearby. If you have a great IT team and employees trust them to help, make sure they are prepared to answer the call. If the supervisor is the go-to guy, arm him or her with the right information.

People Will Find Work-Arounds : pg 159
Take the Employee Perspective : pg 124
Align Your Training With Rewards and Culture : pg 135
Make Sure They're Ready For Day One : pg 24

ANTICIPATE WHAT YOUR TEAM WILL DO ON DAY ONE

1. **Is the old way faster?** They might do what they know, simply to get the job done.

2. **What message is the boss sending?** If she cares only for results and has not demonstrated support for the new method, don't expect the team to change.

3. **What's the consequence for not working the new way?** If there is none, expect noncompliance.

4. **How "real" was the training simulation?** Did the team practice typical scenarios? If not, why expect good performance?

5. **Are you training roles or tools?** If you trained them to use new tools, they'll have to do a lot of mental magic on day one to translate that to their jobs.

6. **Have they learned to handle mistakes?** This is the key to job performance. Training should focus here!

7. **Where do people turn when they need help?** Do what you must to be confident in that support system.

SECTION 3
Engagement

Presentation or Facilitation

"Education is the kindling of a flame,
not the filling of a vessel."

– SOCRATES

We're still learning from Socrates

When most people think of training, they think of a classroom lecture. Participants gain new knowledge by **listening and watching**. This is called **direct information presentation** and most people find it ineffective. The learning just doesn't "stick".

Another approach is the **Socratic Method:** a facilitated dialogue between an expert and new performers. Participants gain new knowledge or skills through **discovery**. Participants go on a journey from one piece of knowledge to the next, creating better understanding and stronger memories. However, this method assumes the learner comes in with some relatable experience on which to build.

Learning is making a connection between the known and the unknown. First, relate the new content to what learners already know. Second, present new concepts to give learners a starting point. Third, facilitate the discovery process.

Strike a balance between telling and facilitating. In the participant's case: between listening and doing.

THINK OF AN EFFECTIVE LEARNING EXPERIENCE YOU'VE HAD

Here's mine:

My driver's ed teacher was a retired military man, his bravery underscored by his position in the passenger seat. He never lost his cool, never swore, but he also didn't talk a lot.

One day, he took us to the steepest hill in town and, one by one, made us coast down the hill and stop the car… *without using our brakes.*

After each student had finished, he asked, "What did you choose to do? Why? What did you do wrong?"

The cocktail of application, the Socratic method, and fear etched the following principles in my mind:
- shift to the lowest gears
- try the emergency brake
- shut the car off, but not altogether, or you could lose steering.

Life-saving learning.

THINK ABOUT AN EFFECTIVE TEACHER YOU'VE HAD

How did the teacher:

Clarify performance expectations and task outcomes?

Explore the boundaries of the situation?

Deliver helpful feedback?

Provide options or suggestions to guide you?

Gain agreement on next steps?

Work in the moment and during formal follow-ups?

PowerPoint is Not Training : pg 36

Use Facilitation In Your Blended Solution : pg 56

Edie Says: **TURN YOUR SUPERVISORS INTO FACILITATORS!**

Help learners discover, outside the training setting. Identify coaches, and equip them to be Socratic. Let me show you how it's done. Imagine I'm a store manager training a new assistant.

EXPECTATIONS So, as I understand it, success for us means you'll be able to confidently open a store — handle security, turn on registers, and conduct a team meeting. Am I on track? What would you add?

BOUNDARIES What worries you about a store opening?

NEXT STEPS When do you want to meet next?

FEEDBACK Whoops — did you see that? If you had pressed F3, your staffing report would have printed accurately.

OPTIONS & FOLLOW-UPS What ideas do you have for your next team meeting? You might also consider....

"You'll see that I incorporated all the points on the previous page. Easy, n'est-ce pas?"

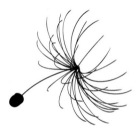

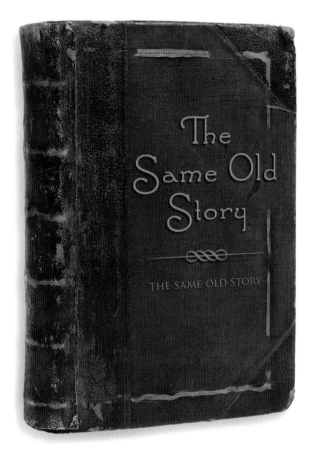

Throughout history, stories have been used to teach. Why don't we use more stories in our learning events? And when we do use them, why are they so bad?

"What do you mean
they're bad?"

Most stories used in training employ two-dimensional characters. The protagonist always does the right thing… or does the wrong thing, has a learning moment, and then tritely accepts his fate. Such stories are not engaging or memorable. Which means they're not helping people learn.

"HOW DO I BUILD A GOOD STORY?"

Let's learn from classic literature and drama.

♦ There's always a protagonist and an antagonist.

♦ The characters are complex – both flawed and sympathetic. They come with backstories that explain how they came to be. They often follow a cultural archetype.

♦ Stories use our emotions to draw us in and keep our attention. Sometimes, music and visual images support the story, involving more of our brains and improving retention.

♦ The story follows a typical arc:

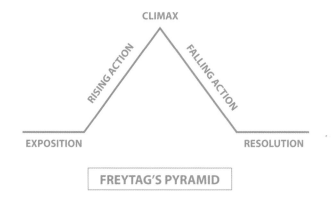

FREYTAG'S PYRAMID

According to Gustav Freytag, a noted dramatist, a story is divided into five parts:

Part 1 | **Exposition** includes background, introductory and setting information

Part 2 | **Rising Action** lays out the basic conflict between the protagonist and his foe

Part 3 | **Climax** presents a fundamental change in the protagonist's situation

Part 4 | **Falling Action** follows the unraveling of conflict, wherein the protagonist wins or loses

Part 5 | **Resolution** describes the protagonist's state (better or worse than at exposition)

"BUT THERE WON'T BE TIME FOR ALL THAT IN TRAINING."

Let's learn from advertising.

- Joe Isuzu
- PC and Mac
- Dos Equis' Most Interesting Man Alive

These characters are established in less than 30 seconds, through images and dialogue, and instructional designers can do the same. Each of the characters has life and dimension. (Joe is a liar, but not a bad guy.) We understand the challenge they face (PC is trying to be cool like Mac.) We know whom we want to emulate. (We should drink whatever the Most Interesting Man drinks.) We get the message.

Now add a bit more story. Imagine the impact of one-minute, well-developed vignettes peppered throughout our training events. Use video, role-plays, storyboards or animation. Let the story carry your content and you can expect a happy ending.

Use Stories to Organize Your Learning Event : pg 17
Does Training Have to Be Boring? : pg 88

Edie Says: "Just look at me! I could have been a series of dry paragraphs, but the authors wisely brought me to life to share my insights on learning. Never fear, dears, I'll arm you with all my most brilliant tips, sharpen your instincts, and maybe even inspire you to be a snappy dresser, like me."

CHARACTER STUDY

In the mid-nineties, Andersen Consulting (now Accenture) put me (Trish) in charge of "deploying a new client service methodology," the thrilling nature of the content captured in those sizzling six words. Historically, the firm communicated new methodology through "talking head" videos of managing partners describing their support, many 3.5 inch binders, and required training. Most of us looked forward to new methodology the way some look forward to chemotherapy. A necessary evil.

This time, our team conspired to deliver content in a way that spoke to the target audience: recent college graduates – smart and cynical weekly travelers with a "work-hard play-hard" mentality. We developed a spokesman character: a large geeky consultant who was frighteningly enthusiastic about methodology, and named him "B.I. Guy" for the Business Integration methodology he adored. We packaged the methodology in small books that consultants could easily carry in a stuffed carry-on. And we embedded Easter eggs (electronic games) in the online tools, as an insider reward designed to create a grassroots pull toward the tools.

At first, management said "No" to B.I. Guy. But we showed rough-cut video vignettes at various meetings and collected reaction data from our target audience. With that, we had the support to make him our official spokesperson.

B.I. Guy was a shocking departure for the firm and, as a result, both loved and hated. Interestingly, according to our data, those in the change management practice roundly rejected him! We suspected it was because they were, at the time, trying hard to gain credibility with their IT counterparts and worried it would undermine their image as serious consultants. One can argue about whether B.I. Guy was successful or not, but he certainly focused attention on a new way of working that was memorable. And fun.

To learn more, see:

Freytag, Gustav. *Freytag's Technique of the Drama: An Exposition of Dramatic Composition and Art.* Translated by Elias J. MacEwan. Charleston: Nabu Press, 2010

"The Top Five Commercial Characters of All Time," blog entry by Charlie Bradley, May 17, 2007, http://www.associatedcontent.com/article/236418/the_top_five_television_commercial.html

Anything written by Dr. Sivasailam Thiagarajan

Does This Have To Be Boring?

Bueller?
Anyone?
Anyone?

We've all experienced this. The teacher or the facilitator that led us straight to a lovely daydream. Thirty minutes later, something jolts us back to reality in time to hear the humdrum of the closing words.

Training does not have to be boring. Boring training is less effective. Learners retain more and perform better when they find the training engaging.

TURN YOUR TRAINING INTO A "DANKE SHOEN" EXPERIENCE

WEAVE IN ACTIVITIES. Activities are inherently less boring than lecture, so err on the side of engagement. Participants who are talking, working, and solving problems are less likely to tune out.

SHARE THE LOAD. Build in ways for participants to learn from each other.

INJECT HUMOR. There's humor in every profession, in every type of situation. Find it and use it. Even your attempts to be funny will be more interesting than a straight delivery of information.

SHOW PASSION! Content doesn't bore people; people do. Do we believe in what we're teaching? Do we think it's important? Show passion! It will rub off on the group.

BE A STORYTELLER. Stories are one of the best vehicles for learning. They are more memorable and they help the learner imagine the right and wrong behaviors. Once you have told your story, ask participants to chime in! They will often have stories that support your content.

DON'T BE THE STAR. Make the training about the content and the learners, not the facilitator.

CO-FACILITATE OR INVITE A GUEST SPEAKER. People often retain more information from several sources.

Edie Says: These tips are the little black dress of instructional design! They work equally well for instructor-led or self-guided learning. Just add pearls!

"You can only have fun
      helping other people have fun
if you're having fun doing it."

– UNKNOWN

Play Works

Training is serious business, right? Right. But using "play" appropriately can boost the effectiveness of your training.

Play has these four characteristics:

- It's voluntary.

- It's intrinsically motivating.

- It involves active engagement, not just listening or answering questions.

- It has a "make believe" aspect.

Intrinsically *what* now?

An intrinsically motivating task is done for its own sake, not because it will be rewarded. To use play in training, you must come up with an activity that's REALLY FUN. Fun, as defined by motivational researchers, means "challenge, curiosity, fantasy, and control."

Does Training Have To Be Boring : pg 88

GAMES PEOPLE PLAY

Take a compelling game, study its structure, tweak it a bit, then use it to meet your learners' objectives.

ELEMENTS OF A COMPELLING GAME	EXAMPLES						
	Bejeweled	Frogger	Solitaire	Charades	Monopoly	Chess	Your Game?
Goal	Next level	Next level	Hand	Being first	Own Property	King	
Time Constraint	Yes	Yes	No	No	No	No	
Randomness/ Surprise	Yes	Yes	Yes	Yes	Go to jail	Opponent's move	
Consequence	Losing	Smoosh	Losing	Losing	Jail	Losing	
Strategy	Yes	Yes	Yes	No	Yes	Yes	
Reward	Jewels move	Move forward	Unload a card	Winning	Houses / Hotels	Capturing & gaining position	
Movement/ Manipulatives	Yes	Yes	Yes	Yes	Yes	Yes	
Competition	House	House	House	Others	Others	Other	

ID ROADKILL: A FRAMEWORK

Each team has three minutes to answer the question under the post-it. Answer correctly to progress to the next level. **Goal:** get to mastery.

GO FOR THE FLOW

So you do incorporate play into your learning events? Great. Now optimize the effects of play.

Learn about the Flow Theory of Optimal Experience (Mihaly Csikszentmihalyi, 1990). "Flow" gets its name from the word people use to describe the state they're in when they're entirely absorbed and making progress against an objective. They feel so engaged that they seem to be pulled along without effort through the activity.

What you're going for, as a designer, is an activity that qualifies as "play," and also:

- provides clear goals
- gives clear feedback on progress
- optimizes challenge
- absorbs the learner
- offers the learner a feeling of control

Done right, participants become less self-conscious and actually lose track of time. The state is characterized by a lack of boredom and a lack of anxiety.

If you're thinking about gaming right now, you're on the right track. Setting your content in the context of a virtual world is a great way to achieve all the requirements of play and to target that "flow" that helps learners break new ground.

Edie Says: **GAMES TO RETIRE**

Psst… can we make a pact? Let's agree to never subject our participants to Jeopardy, Koosk, Build Something, or Let's Go Around the Room again? These games are the dripping faucet of training. Aren't we capable of more?

To learn more, see:

Rieber, Lloyd P. "Seriously considering play: Designing interactive learning environments based on the blending of microworlds, simulations, and games." *Educational Technology Research & Development, 44*(2) (1996): 43-58.

Make Your
Training a Day
at the Beach

In **The Change Book**, we reference a terrific article by Drake Bennett called The Best Vacation Ever. In it, he builds on research from psychology, economics and behavioral economics to discuss how people derive pleasure from their vacations.

"….how long we take off probably counts for less than we think, and in the aggregate, taking more short trips leaves us happier than taking a few long ones. We're often happier planning a trip than actually taking it. And interrupting a vacation – far from being a nuisance – can make us enjoy it more. How a trip ends matters more than how it begins, who you're with matters as much as where you go, and if you want to remember a vacation vividly, do something during it that you've never done before. And though it may feel unnecessary, it's important to force yourself to actually take the time off in the first place – people, it turns out, are as prone to procrastinate when it comes to pleasurable things like vacations as unpleasant ones like paperwork and visits to the dentist." – Drake Bennett

Those of us interested in creating a memorable learning experience can benefit from the principles Drake Bennett presents.

ANTICIPATION: We enjoy looking forward to an experience more than actually experiencing it. Instructional designers should consider what we can do to heighten this response.

INTENSITY: We remember intense highs or lows, and novelty – the "Peak-End" rule. If we want to create a truly memorable experience, we should create short programs that end with a positive, novel experience. Recency is a factor here as well – the last experience, whether it was positive or negative, colors the impression of the overall program.

PARTITIONING: If our positive experience is interrupted by reality, we actually enjoy it more. This suggests building shorter training sessions scattered through the work experience rather than an intensive three-week boot camp.

DEADLINES: We tend to procrastinate on activities with an extended deadline. Set short time frames for training registration and completion.

reference | Bennett, Drake. "The Best Vacation Ever." *The Boston Globe* June 20, 2010, http://www.boston.com/bostonglobe/ideas/ articles/2010/06/20/the_best_vacation_ever/

The Five Most
Hated Words...

"LET'S GO AROUND THE ROOM AND I'D LIKE EACH OF YOU TO TELL THE GROUP...

- ♦ your name and the group you're from.
- ♦ what you hope to get out of this class.
- ♦ one problem you'd like to discuss.
- ♦ a surprising fact about you."

Is there a more **tired, expected, unimaginative** thing to ask your participants?

"BUT WHAT'S WRONG WITH IT?"

- ♦ People expect it.
- ♦ It makes them nervous.
- ♦ It feels forced, unnatural and uncomfortable.
- ♦ It takes forever.
- ♦ Participants often tune out and lose most of the information they hear.

"YEAH, EXCEPT THAT IT GETS PEOPLE TALKING, GIVES ME INFORMATION, CONFIRMS LEARNING OBJECTIVES, IDENTIFIES EXPERTISE IN THE ROOM, BEGINS RELATIONSHIPS BETWEEN PARTICIPANTS..."

Great goals. Let's find a better way to make those things happen.

AROUND THE ROOM IS SO FIVE MINUTES AGO

Is the session online? Does everyone show up with a laptop? Set up a **chat room**. Type a question to the group, and let everyone in the classroom type their responses, so all can see and read them. Make it interactive by calling out interesting responses and asking individuals to elaborate.

Are participants computer-literate? Do you have technical support for your training? Then try using **social networking** concepts. For example, some time before the session, you might send learners a fake Facebook page as a template. Have them fill out their "pages" with all the information you asked for, submit the pages to you ahead of time, then upload before the start of class. Let participants spend 30 minutes reading pages and interacting – getting to know each other – either online or face-to-face. This is even better if your organization uses a real social networking tool. You could also use a public social network that's used for professional purposes (for example, LinkedIn).

Low tech? Have participants do some **flipchart prep**. Each person should show up with one flipchart page including all the information you want: name, group, role, areas of expertise, and fun fact. Post the flipchart pages around the room, read them, then ask certain individuals to talk about themselves or their experiences.

Want to take the pressure off them? Do a **roll call**. Prepare yourself with information about your participants. Then YOU go around the room and ask each one a probing question, which will serve as their introduction to the group.

Do you want to identify expertise in the room? Ask for a volunteer for each subject area, then do some **professional speed dating**. Set your experts at different stations and have the rest of the participants rotate from one station to the next, introducing themselves and asking the "expert" questions.

striving for elevated realization
logistically efficient
sub-optimal output
predicated on sound utilization of
TPS, AMRAKs,BRP, MRP, MBR

Speak to Learners in Their Native Tongue

There are three nasties that want in to your training and communications, and their names are **Acronym, Made-up** and **Flowery.**

Acronyms and abbreviations are everywhere, so don't encourage them. If an acronym is already part of day-to-day language, use it. But otherwise, have mercy! New acronyms have to be decoded, and that takes mental work.

Made-Up words are terms and euphemisms coined for the change initiative. People have to learn these new words to understand your training and the new way of working. Again, extra effort.

Flowery sounds pretty, but she's not. Every extra syllable or complex word clings to your text, weighing it down and hiding your message.

"But the team designed the (system, tool, initiative, job) with these new words. So now we have to use them!" Right, but you're the expert on the people side of the change. Make a case for stripping out the nonsense, where you can. And next time, insist that the development team use plain English (or your spoken language). Use the word "usability;" they like that one.

The IT team members often are comfortable with them; management might love the spin new words put on a tough-but-necessary transition. Help them see that their words are not helping achieve their objective and smooth adoption of the change. The easier it is for people to understand, the more readily they will do it.

"Oh… 'meltdown'. It's one of those annoying buzzwords. We prefer to call it an unrequested fission surplus."

– MR. BURNS, "THE SIMPSONS"

"As part of the contract approval process, agencies must submit an ECR (RC215) or PO (RC744) with the appropriate encumbrance of funds. Immediately following the approval of the contract, the encumbrance will be recorded in the CDs against the appropriation from which contract commitments will be paid. Once recorded, state departments and agencies must not reduce the contract encumbrance, except when the estimated liability for the fiscal year is reduced.

In some cases, agencies are permitted to data-enter contract encumbrances in the CDs and these must be recorded only in sequence of contract submissions. In the event that a contract is disapproved, the related contract encumbrance will be cancelled by PRB."

[Paragraph paraphrased from a financial training manual. Acronyms have been changed to protect the misguided.]

Taking the User's Perspective is About More Than Words : pg 124
That's a Training Issue. Is It? : pg 128

"Short words are best
and the old words when short
are best of all."

– WINSTON CHURCHILL

In 1998, the band *Love and Rockets* released a song, "RIP 20 C," consisting only of abbreviations. There was a contest to find the first person who knew the meaning of all 69.

THE POINT?

Decoding abbreviations and acronyms is work.

FIRST VERSE OF "RIP 20 C" ▶

RIP KGB CIA JUD FDA LSD FBI

MT ROM PCP UDA FCC KKK

MAD CNN BBC EMI THC ICI TNT

NR MDA SAS JFK RAM CND

RS LED HBO GHB YSL RIP RIP

TO ABC RPM CNC MIT IRA EEC

RH KFC IBM HIV VCR VAT PLF

BC MGM ANC MOR MTV AAA

RT ATM TAZ DAR XTC FAA VIP

BS CID RAF DDT DOM DAT TVC

EDU FO GOD US ARIP RIP RIP

Performance

Training Is
Not an Event

It's a process.
And it's not just "training."

Achieving a behavior change requires many solutions, used over time.

✓ Think of learning and development as a collection of tools that create and buttress desired behavior.

Instructional designers are the architects of learning and development experiences.

Learning Begins When Training Ends : pg 63
Use A Blended Solution : pg 56

THE ARCHITECTURE

COMMUNITIES OF PRACTICE

MENTORING

VISUAL CUEING

PERFORMANCE APPRAISAL

REWARDS

FORMAL LEARNING

PERFORMANCE SUPPORT

ON-THE-JOB TRAINING

JOB AIDS

COACHING

KNOWLEDGE MANAGEMENT

EXPERTS

JOB ASSIGNMENTS

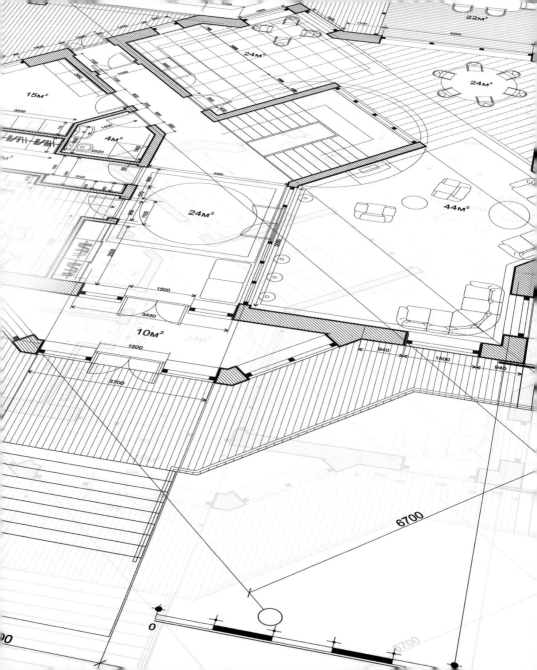

Take the
Learner's
Perspective

Remember that old saying "put yourself in my shoes"?

It's absolutely essential when creating a learning solution.

Think about each role represented in your audience. Gather enough information from the right sources so that you can imagine yourself in their shoes. Or in their chairs.

1. What are the most important parts of their jobs? What behaviors drive business results?

2. What is their motivation? What are they rewarded for? What are they punished for?

3. What kinds of behaviors are supported or discouraged by company culture?

4. What are their work settings? Group? Solitary? Loud? Quiet? Long periods of work or lots of switching gears?

5. What language, acronyms and metaphors do they use? What kinds of communication and support make sense to them?

6. How do they feel about the change? What will their attitudes and expectations be as they begin to learn?

WHY IS THIS SO IMPORTANT?

Because we want our solution to be realistic and usable. Without it, we might be training to behaviors that our audience will simply not perform or using a method to which they're not receptive. By putting ourselves in their shoes, we have a chance at creating a learning solution that will really shine.

Speak to Users in Their Native Tongue : pg 111
Align Training With Culture and Rewards : pg 153

That's a Training Issue. Is It?

So often we hear on our projects, "That's a training issue." Unfortunately, more often than not, the issue cannot be solved with training.

To get to the true performance problem, we have to find the root cause. Many of these root causes are buried deep within the organization and the "training issue" is just a symptom. Identifying the root cause is the only way to solve the problem for good.

Edie Says: Friends, my handbags and my shoes always match. And I only offer training for skill/knowledge problems.

HOUSTON, WE HAVE A PROBLEM.

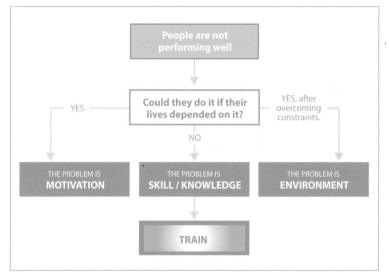

BY ENVIRONMENT, WE MEAN ANYTHING EXTERNAL TO THE PERFORMER:

- ♦ **Product or Service**
- ♦ **Reward System**
- ♦ **Business Process**
- ♦ **IT Solution**
- ♦ **Client or Vendor Relationships**
- ♦ **Communication**

GET DOWN ON IT.
FIND THE ROOT CAUSE.

ISOLATED OR SYSTEMIC

Determine if what you see is an exceptional event or part of a larger set of problems.

THE FIVE WHYs

Ask yourself why something is happening five times. Most times you'll find the root cause.

FOLLOW THE IMPACTS

Figure out whether a proposed solution might lead to other problems. The other problems might be your clue to the root cause.

Make Sure It's Not a Lack of Good Information : pg 17
Training Is Not an Event, It's a Process : pg 120
A Blended Solution : pg 56

An industrial manufacturing company wanted to improve customer service. They had never offered formal training before, so training appeared to be an obvious solution.

But when the instructional designer went to the floor here's what she found: employees had to use three separate systems to process a customer request. Each system had a unique interface, separate processes and different codes. Employees had to toggle from one system to another, and in some cases walk from one terminal to another. They had to remember information or write it down – all to translate it, and then reenter it!

The instructional designer realized training would never allow employees to work more effectively or productively. This was an IT and process problem!

The Cheese

Any rat in the lab will tell you: you do what gets you the cheese.

For the rat, it's finding the right path in the maze, or pressing the right lever.

The motivators that shape people's behavior are more complex, but no less powerful. They run the spectrum of Maslow's hierarchy: safety to self-actualization.

The set of expectations implicit in any organization is often called its "culture." People are strongly compelled to behave in ways that fit the culture.

The set of explicit rules and incentives to behave is often called the "reward system." People want more rewards (pay, promotions, perks) and few punishments (sanctions, negative reviews, demotion, loss of power). Newly trained behaviors will not succeed if the culture and reward system do not support them. They will not run away from the cheese.

What if we try to train behaviors that are **contrary** to culture and rewards? Behaviors that don't get anybody any cheese? We fail.

WHAT'S THE CULTURE OF YOUR ORGANIZATION?

Rebels? Armies of one? Individual stardom? Breaking away from the pack?

One big family? Cooperation and synergy? A band of brothers who have each other's back?

Creators and innovators? Thinking outside the box? Dazzling the team with new ideas? Daring to fail?

WHAT ARE PEOPLE REWARDED FOR IN YOUR ORGANIZATION?

What gets them high evaluations, promotions, more money or recognition?

Speed? Quality? Leadership? Expertise? Customer service?

 Put Yourself in the Learner's Shoes : pg 124

Edie Says:

A CERTAIN HEALTH INSURANCE AGENCY HIRED NEW COLLEGE GRADUATES TO BE CUSTOMER SERVICE REPRESENTATIVES WHO SOLVED PROBLEMS! AND THEY TRAINED THEM WITH THAT GOAL IN MIND. HOWEVER, THE AGENCY NEVER CHANGED HOW THEY MEASURED CSR BEHAVIOR: NUMBER OF CALLS TAKEN PER HOUR. HMMM. I WONDER HOW MANY PROBLEMS WERE SOLVED?

STEAMERS COFFEE wanted more information to try to optimize sales and promotions. They built a new online tool to collect sales information periodically throughout the day. They also wanted qualitative data, so they asked managers to post customer behavior information twice per shift.

Managers were brought in for a half-day training session, where they learned the new tool and discussed how the information would help the company retain its position as market leader. Nearly every manager completed training activities successfully.

A month after rollout, the results were in: management called the program a failure. The reason? Store managers were missing posting windows, or not posting at all. The qualitative data they provided was sparse and largely unusable.

WHY?

Steamers was all about customer relationships. Their brand was not "big chain", but rather a series of independent, neighborhood coffee shops. Store managers were promoted and compensated for repeat business, customer feedback and customer loyalty. They thrived on relationships with regulars and hosted community events to bring in new business. Managers and associates were hired for their outgoing, warm, and sometimes quirky personalities. They took pride in knowing the orders of regulars, before they ordered. Periodically, senior managers visited stores to observe the "vibe" first hand.

Given that, managers had no incentive to sit in the back office for half an hour, twice a day, entering data into spreadsheets and typing descriptions of their customer interactions. The situation came to a head at one store during a headquarters visit when the HQ project lead addressed the store manager with an air of unpleasant duty. "Why haven't you been filling out your reports?" The store manager replied, "That's easy. There are no customers in my office!"

SMEs Operate
in Cruise Control

Don't let them drive

Subject Matter Experts (SMEs) have something called "unconscious competence." They are so good at what they do that they don't know how or why they do it. Many of the smartest things they do are done without a thought.

Why would we ask someone who can't describe how they perform a task to train someone else? We shouldn't.

Also, because of their extreme expertise, it's hard for them to put themselves in the shoes of the new learner.

So they don't know all the steps, and they can't relate to training participants. Not a recipe for success.

We need SMEs. They provide the content for our learning experiences, credibility with our audience, and answers to the toughest questions. But in the classroom? Let a professional drive.

THE BEST USES FOR A SME IN THE CLASSROOM:

♦ Answering technical questions
♦ Validating content
♦ Providing examples
♦ Endorsing the change

TIPS FOR CO-FACILITATING

If you do ask a SME to train for you, partner him or her with an experienced facilitator.

BEFORE THE SESSION

Decide who does what.

Plan a shared message.

Learn each other's sections for backup.

Discuss situations when your partner may signal to you to take over.

DURING THE SESSION

Explain why you are co-facilitating.

Have the co-facilitator sit in view of participants.

Don't correct each other.

Ask for the other's input.

SMEs PROVIDE INPUT TO AND VALIDATE ACCURACY OF TRAINING MATERIALS.

SMEs DO NOT VALIDATE INSTRUCTIONAL DESIGN.

RESPONSIBILITIES OF SMEs

- Identify learner characteristics.

- Provide content resources for training materials.

- Describe realistic business situations to bring the content to life.

- Provide real-life examples, non-examples and mistakes.

- Meet all review and project timelines.

- Review and approve content accuracy.

- Sustain project deliverables post go-live.

- Advocate for training.

Speak to Users in Their Native Tongue : pg 111
Take the User's Perspective : pg 124

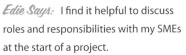

Edie Says: I find it helpful to discuss roles and responsibilities with my SMEs at the start of a project.

Set the Bar Higher

Research shows that some students actually perform better than other students simply because they are *expected to do so*.

✓ *Performance in training and on the job can be influenced by the expectations of others.*

Pretty powerful, right? So how do you do this properly? There are two methods, used either in a learning session or on the job: Stretch Goals and Action Learning.

"If you think you can do a thing
or think you can't do a thing,
you're right."

– HENRY FORD

SET STRETCH GOALS

- **Stretch Goals are named "Stretch" because they are very difficult to meet.** If the standard is achievable by most of your class or work group, it's not a Stretch Goal.

- **Stretch Goals are not goals that people are required or expected to meet.** So don't punish people for not achieving them.

- **Performance against stretch targets can affect other parts of the organization.** If employees start becoming much more efficient or increasing output, they'll change something about the business process. Know the upstream and downstream impacts of changing employee behavior.

- **Provide people with the knowledge, tools, and means to meet Stretch Goals, or the effects can be disastrous.** If no one can meet the goal because of lack of support or resources, it has the opposite effect on motivation, productivity and teamwork.

- **Reward people for taking risks, even if they fail.** One company builds failure expectations into performance reviews – they expect one significant slip-up per year. This beautifully complements action learning – studying one's own actions and experience in order to improve performance.

ACTION LEARNING

When employees deal with actual business issues, there are real consequences for failure. People are more focused and productive, and they learn from the experience more easily. The challenge for trainers is to bring some of that urgency to the classroom. The more relevant and realistic the training, the more participants learn.

- **Create an experience that is highly engaging**, and mimics the tasks of "real work." Pick a highly realistic training scenario – a situation that adds real value to the organization. Make sure the setting, tools, inputs and outputs are as close as possible to a real work situation.

- **Debrief the experience** – review process, behavior, performance and results. This step is critical to action learning. Participants examine their actions and the results so that they understand how best to improve outcomes in the future.

- **Generalize from results** – what does this mean for the organization? What will the effects be on customers, team performance, Key Performance Indicators, the work of other departments and external entities?

- **Transfer lessons to the future.** Put in place ways for participants to apply the learning on the job.

GETTING HUMANS TO THE MOON IN
TEN YEARS WAS A STRETCH GOAL

It was set for the U.S. by President Kennedy in the 1960s even though, at the time, it was not yet technically feasible. NASA achieved their stretch goal through action learning. The teams at NASA built on each success and each failure, learning at a blistering rate and improving their performance to the point that they met their goal.

Today? There are environmentalists who want to see the death of the combustible engine in the next ten years. It seems implausible, but so did walking on the moon.

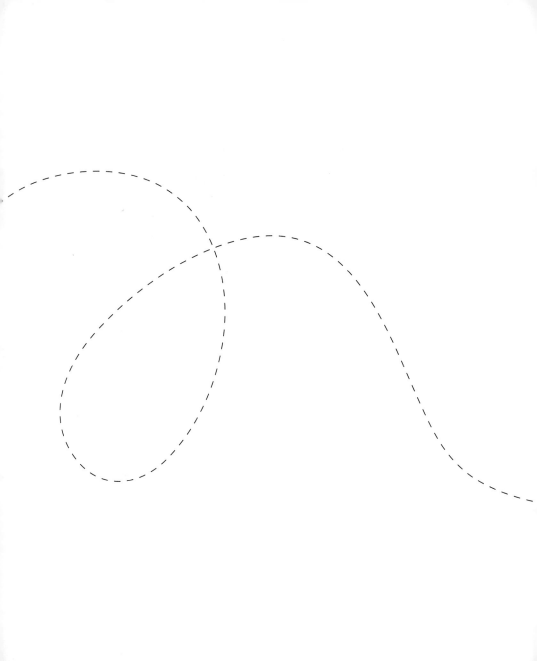

Can a Fly
Help a Company
Save Money?

It depends on your business

If you run a janitorial service, it sure can. Research has shown that a fly painted on a men's urinal can save 85% in cleaning costs. It turns out that men do a better job not missing if they have something to aim at.

You see, *performance will happen*. It will happen whether you guide it or not. You might as well shape it into something that works for the organization.

Men use urinals. The janitorial service wants accurate, cleaner delivery to reduce the time and amount of cleaning product.

As learning and development professionals, we want the same thing: accurate and repeatable performance.

We have three options to help guide performance in the right direction:

DESIGN | Modify the system/processes to guide performance in the right way.

SUPPORT | Provide references and aids to allow the learner to perform as prescribed.

LEARNING | Create a learning event to train the learner how to perform properly.

IS PERFORMANCE SUPPORT RIGHT FOR YOU?

If you answer 'yes' to most of these questions, job aids and/or performance support might be right for you.

- Do you have a large audience (over 250)?
- Is your audience dispersed?
- Is the content complex so that you couldn't know it all by heart?
- Is the task performed infrequently?
- Does management support new ways of learning?
- Are there high consequences for errors?
- Would performers benefit from advice while performing?

Training Is Not An Event : pg 120
Learning Begins When Training Ends : pg 63
Learn Why the Medium Matters : pg 49
Use A Blended Approach : pg 56
Play Works : pg 95

reference | Cross, Jay. *Informal Learning.* San Francisco: Pfeiffer, 2006.

To learn more, see:

Rossett, Allison. Job Aids and Performance Support: Moving From Knowledge in the Classroom to Knowledge Everywhere. San Francisco: Pfeiffer, 2006.

Harless, Joseph H. *"Guiding Performance with Job Aids," Introduction to Performance Technology,* ISPI (1986).

Employees *Will* Find a Workaround

MAYBE WE SHOULD JUST TAKE AWAY EXCEL

A major clothing retailer was in the process of implementing a new financial planning system for their merchandise buys. For the third time.

Close to "go live," employees staged a near revolt. Sponsors disappeared into the shadows. People were too busy for training. Users complained that the system was too slow and difficult.

The CEO and CFO responded with a mandate: like it or not, everyone must use this system! And they did, for a short time.

As part of the rollout, the project team trained "super users" – experts who advocated for the system back in the business units.

Or not. In reality, these super users became clever creators of work-arounds – new tools that extracted data from the system, dumped it into Excel, and allowed users to do work the old way.

THE RESULT

There was an integrated and centralized financial planning system – that employees must use – which started the pipeline.

Reporting was cumbersome and inefficient. Data was exported to Excel, formatted and manipulated based on department, not company, needs.

Some periodic management processes never happened because IT was pulled to create Excel tools.

THE MORAL

As part of an overall change effort, the team should have focused on training the critical, common and catastrophic. Through a series of layered successes, users might have better understood the new system's potential, and become contributors to making it work.

"Resistance is futile."

– THE BORG

Prevent workarounds

Give them a good system! Processes and tools that work meet less resistance.

Train the critical, common and catastrophic.

Practice, practice, practice on the new system or process.

Reward team experts – the heroes who help the struggling and rejected masses.

Find the rough spots. There might be additional work for some employees. These areas might need a little training boost.

Identify one to three simple ways for people to experience immediate success. If they perceive the new process works, they'll use it.

Train This: **Critical, Common, Catastrophic** : pg 8
Learning Begins Where Training Ends : pg 63

The Case for Place

Imagine trying to learn how to fly an airplane in a classroom. The instructor told you everything you need to know – lift, thrust, rolls, yaw, yins, yangs, whizzes and bangs. Now you're behind the stick of a 747 loaded with passengers, on your way to JFK. Preposterous, right?

Why? Well, in order for us to perform in the real world, we need to transfer what we learned in the class to actual performance. The further the learning environment is from the performance environment, the less likely it is that the learner will transfer what they learned to the real world.

"State-dependent learning" says people perform better in the physical environment in which they learned to perform. That includes all the sights, sounds, smells, tools and people. So, ideally, the learner would receive training in his or her performance environment – **the real workspace**.

Sometimes it's not practical to practice in the real world. You can't take a novice pilot and let him or her fly a 747. But pilot trainers know the importance of state-dependent learning. Their trainees go through hours of simulation in a **realistic environment** with equipment and sensory feedback that mimic the real thing.

BUT YOU CAN'T TRAIN IN A
REAL WORK SETTING. RIGHT?

"I can't have people take training where they work every day."
Why not? If there's a shared workspace, try setting up an "instant class-room." Or, if that's logistically impossible, do a presentation nearby and then some facilitated practice at their desks or work areas. Or bolster classroom training with self-guided lessons available online or on the job, so employees learn using their own computers or work facilities.

"I can't let them interact with real customers or clients until they're ready!" Why not? Selected clients might welcome the chance to help you improve your service to them. Or have seasoned employ-ees role-play customers or submit customer problems or calls. Also, consider the buddy system. Let learners shadow experienced peers as they do their real jobs, and then switch; have the peers monitor the learners' first interactions with real customers.

THE GOAL :

Speed to performance

"We can't have them messing around in our live systems."
Why not? Control it, supervise it and allow it in small doses. Or set up a training environment or simulation that feels exactly like the real one.

"I can't have the team at training, all at once." Why not? Schedule training off-hours, with compensation or incentives for attending. Or train part of the team and let the others cover for them. At least learners will have some real-life teammates with them as they learn.

THERE'S REAL AND THEN THERE'S REAL DANGEROUS

The FBI's Hogan's Alley is a great example of a realistic training environment. When we were consultants to the FBI, we occasionally had meetings there. But there were times we were delayed, because we weren't allowed in when trainees were practicing shooting at each other. We thought that was a very reasonable rule.

"The Firehouse" is the training facility where learners can use live ammunition. One of our FBI teammates told us a funny story. (Funny to us, anyway.) Apparently, there's a catwalk between rooms in one of the buildings. A couple trainees were completing an exercise. They broke down a door, had to assess whether the mannequins and cardboard people were "good" or "bad," shoot the bad ones, then break through to the next room. As they dashed into the next room, they set off a flashbang, which stunned and incapacitated the onlookers on the catwalk…. who happened to be a couple of visiting foreign dignitaries.

WHAT ELSE CAN IMPROVE TRANSFER?

Plan follow-up activities. Provide activities to be completed on the job that reinforce what was learned in training.

Ask the manager to conduct a training debrief. When an employee's manager asks him or her questions about what he or she learned, the employee will be more likely to retain it and apply it to the job.

Schedule learning when it is needed. The less time between learning and real-world performance, the more learning will be transferred to the job.

Chunk it. The more complex information presented at one time, the less will be retained. Sequence learning units over time.

Provide the "What's in it for me?" (WIIFM). Learners need to know how they'll benefit from what they're learning. Provide it up front and reinforce it throughout the program.

REFLECTION

Emergency situations are the toughest to train. Imagine how you would devise realistic activities for these situations. How would you teach a:

SALES ASSOCIATE - HOW TO DEAL WITH BLOOD-BORNE PATHOGENS IN A FITTING ROOM.

SCHOOL TEACHER - HOW TO PUT OUT A SMALL FIRE IN HIS ROOM.

GAS STATION ATTENDANT - HOW TO MANAGE A SMALL GAS SPILL.

FERRY BOAT CAPTAIN - HOW TO MANAGE A BOAT THAT IS TAKING ON WATER.

BUS DRIVER - HOW TO HANDLE A HOSTAGE SITUATION ON THE BUS.

Take the User Perspective : pg 124
Learning Begins When Training Ends : pg 63

Use It
or
Lose It

$$\left(-a\right) = -\frac{c}{a}$$

$$\left(x + \frac{b}{2a}\right)^2 = -\frac{c}{a} + \frac{c}{4a}$$

$$\left(x + \frac{b}{2a}\right)^2 = \frac{b^2 - 4ac}{4a^2}$$

$$x + \frac{b}{2a} = \pm \frac{}{4ac}$$

$$x = -b +$$

Are you ready to solve for x or calculate the sin θ for an angle? Probably not.

Unless you work with these formulas on a regular basis, you won't feel prepared to solve for x. But you used to use these formulas to ace your algebra exams.

So why can't you solve algebraic equations anymore? The culprit is called "lack of use."

Forgetting an algebraic equation is not important to most people. But lack of use is a big deal for organizations. It's one of the top reasons companies don't realize the benefits of their learning investments.

TRAINING INVESTMENT
+ PRACTICE

SKILLS, KNOWLEDGE AND BUSINESS RESULTS

You can have the best training program in the world, but if participants don't immediately apply what they learned on the job, they will lose it – along with your training investment.

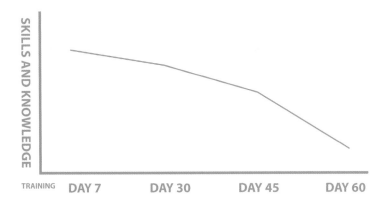

Ability to remember what was learned in the class decreases over time.

KEEP THOSE SKILLS FRESH

1. **Extend the learning experience** – design a program that has a learning event (classroom, online or virtual session) AND post-learning-event activities (check-ins, on-the-job challenges, learning networks), encouraging participants to use their new skills after "training" is over.

2. **Involve managers** – give managers a role in the learning experience and hold them accountable for ensuring their direct reports CAN and DO apply new skills.

3. **Make it real** – integrate those post-training behaviors into the official performance goals and rewards for employees and managers.

4. **Use just-in-time training** – train only what is immediately needed or what will be immediately used on the job.

Learning is a Process : pg 120
Make Sure You Get the Right Performance on the Job : pg 153
People Keep Learning After Training Ends : pg 63
Training Was A Success? How Do You Know? : pg 24

Edie Says: You're a professional. You knew how to develop strong learning programs before you even cracked this book. But everyone – yes, even moi – needs inspiration once in awhile. My goal for you, darlings, is that you deliver stellar results without breaking a sweat. I hope this book has helped!

ABOUT THE AUTHORS

Trish Emerson has spent her career managing organizational change. Her passion is helping enhance the value of her clients' most important asset—their people. Trish so loves her chosen field that she launched her own firm: Emerson Human Capital Consulting, Inc. (EHC). Since 2001, EHC has provided organizations with creative solutions that bring tangible results.

Trish spends her free time maintaining her Victorian home in Alameda, California with her husband, while entertaining their son, an intrepid cat, and a constant stream of house guests.

Mary Stewart loves to talk about change. A former Big Five change management consultant, Mary now considers herself a writer and communicator. She has found her groove helping Emerson Human Capital reach out to clients and the consulting industry. She helps craft messages to clients, maintains EHC's branding and image, and supports the communication line of business.

Mary loves her work, but her true passions are raising her three children, finding and feeding two elusive cats, and spending time with her big, extended family in Oak Park, Illinois.